The Possibility Factor
Prayer Journal

Also By LaTania Michelle

The Possibility Factor,
Your guide to believing anything is
possible for you.

଼ାୠ

Advance Praise for *The Possibility Factor Prayer Journal*

"LaTania Michelle is a forceful woman of destiny! She is a visionary motivator firmly rooted in her relationship with our Lord Jesus Christ which exudes onto her captive listeners. A profound prayer leader strategically stationed in the body of Christ for such a time as this. LaTania is part of a continuing generational legacy of prayer warriors which includes her Father, Mother, siblings and extends to her daughter as well. She has a delightful ability to walk you into your victorious place in God. I consider her my spiritual life coach and I invite you to allow the pages of this book to inspire you towards God's best for you." Cheryl Foley

℘℣

"I truly believe after reading **The Possibility Factor Prayer Journal**, that LaTania has given us the key to unlock the door to receiving God's unlimited blessings for our lives. In her teachings we find the pre-requisites to manifest God's good and perfect will. I have been blessed and encouraged through reading the confessions, and prayers, as well as my faith, has increased tremendously.

After reading this book, I have come to the conclusion that I can accomplish my dreams and goals through the confession of the word and daily communication with God. This prayer journal is a must have in order to effectively pray and achieve success and God's purpose for your life." Kimselff – Author, Speaker

ഇൗരു

"Ms. LaTania Smith is a powerful woman of God. LaTania brings hope to a hopeless world. Her book is a testimony to keeping the faith and overcoming seemingly insurmountable obstacles. She speaks life into dead situations. Ms. Smith encourages others to hold onto their dreams and the promises of God. LaTania is an example of what faith and determination and never giving up can do; she is a dream birther."
Rita Hall, Author of ***Ebony Bitter-Sweet; A Chocolate Girl in a Vanilla World***

ഇൗരു

"Through prayer & faith, LaTania has been able to inspire & encourage the greatest & the least, on to accomplish great things in the kingdom & the world; even the impossible. With this book, She has been able to simply & concisely give us all what we need to take our intimate relationship with God, as well as the Great Power that comes with it to the next level. I am excited for all you readers, LaTania has helped me change my life for the better & now she will help you." Roberto Hayes – Senior Pastor, Power of The Holy Spirit International

₨₩

"LaTania Michelle is a force of nature, the nature of goodness in a turbulent world. Her calm and steady voice becomes a beacon in your consciousness to choose faith over folly, Christ over false gods and truth over lies. Her knowledge of the Bible is awe-inspiring to me and I count her among my friends that I hold close to my heart, for I know she lives with God first in her life."

Maureen O'Crean, co-author, *I Am Diva, Every Woman's Guide to Outrageous Living* and founder of Distinctively Diva.

₨₩

The
Possibility Factor

Prayer Journal

Your 30 Day Journey
From Impossibility to Victory!

LaTania Michelle

Distinctively Diva Press
Los Angeles

Distinctively Diva Press

Distinctively Diva
703 Pier Avenue, Ste B, #309
Hermosa Beach, CA 90254
www.distincitivelydiva.com

ISBN: 978-09799902-2-9

Limits of Liability and Disclaimer of Warranty

The author and publisher shall not be liable for your misuse of this material. This book is strictly for informational and educational purposes.

Scriptures are from the New King James Version

Warning – Disclaimer

The purpose of this book is to educate and entertain. The author and/or publisher do not guarantee that anyone following these techniques, suggestions, tips, ideas, or strategies will become successful. The author and/or publisher shall have neither liability nor responsibility to anyone with respect to any loss or damage caused, or alleged to be caused, directly or indirectly by the information contained in this book.

Presented To

By

Occasion

Dedication

T his prayer journal is dedicated to all of the Saturday morning prayer call intercessors. You are a great, mighty and blessed group of men and women.

Your faithfulness to pray for me, one another, our nation and the body of Christ has encouraged my faith to new levels in the Lord and strengthened my spiritual walk in ways you will never know. We have truly seen God turn impossible situations around and because of you, many lives have been changed and souls have been saved.

I love all of you, and I pray for each of you daily. I pray that God will continue to manifest his loving kindness in your life. Thank you for all of your love and support.

The word says that the faithful man shall abound with blessings. You guys definitely qualify for this promise. So be blessed in every way and always remember that "Nothing Shall Be Impossible For You Because You Are Believers."

Special Thanks

Thank you,
Mommy for your prayers and wisdom and for always believing in me, your encouragement has made the difference in my life.

Thank you,
Jasmine for your patience, love and support you are the inspiration for all that I do.

Thank you,
Shiralyn Ellerbe my older, wiser sister you have been a constant source of wisdom, encouragement and prayer.

Thank you,
Minister Eric Dixon, you have been so wonderful. I love you and I am thankful for your love and support. You are a true man of God.

Thank you,
Maureen O'Crean, my friend, my mentor and prayer partner. Thank you for always keeping my head in the game.

ॐ

You Are Never Given A Passion

Without The Ability To Pursue It

You Are Never Given A Purpose

Without The Promise To Fulfill It

You Are Never Given A Dream

Without The Power To

Make It Come True!

By

LaTania Michelle

ॐ

My Prayer For You

Dear Heavenly Father,

I lift up to you the person who is reading this book right now. I ask you Lord to cover their heart and mind with the blood of Jesus. Give them a new hunger and thirst for seeking you in your word, spending time with you in prayer and loving you by loving others with your agape.

Lord, please touch this reader and fill their heart and mind with hope so that they can freely dream again. Heal them Father and remove all disappointment, pain and fear from their heart.

Dear Lord, please place your love, peace and joy deep within their soul and strengthen them to courageously believe in you for great things to happen in their lives. Reveal the greatness of your love. Show them your loving kindness and crown them with glory and honor. Reveal the dreams you have placed in their heart. Cause them to dream again, dream big and give birth to the impossible in their lives.

In Jesus Name
Amen

Introduction

Mark 9:23
"Jesus said to him, 'If you can believe, all things are possible to him who believes'."

Matthew 19:26
"But Jesus looked at them and said to them, 'With men this is impossible, but with God all things are possible'."

"With God all things are possible." "All things are possible to him who believes." Jesus Himself made this announcement several times in the scripture. Jesus taught His disciples the two factors needed to do the impossible. With God and by faith all things are possible. In Luke 18:27 Jesus also said, *"The things which are impossible with men are possible with God."*

These are very familiar verses. But the truth is we have been so conditioned by society, our environment and our past mistakes that we have subtly denied the power of God's word to turn our impossible situations around.

Ask yourself have you limited God in anyway?

- The media reports the country is in an economic recession. So, instead of believing that God can supernaturally bless your business or give you a better job, you decide to scale back and settle for barely getting by.

- Because of your credit score you are denied a home loan so instead of increasing your faith to own a home you replace your dreams of home ownership with an apartment on the nice side of town.
- The recent statistics states that women over a certain age are less likely to get married so instead of believing God for a loving, faithful, supportive mate you give up your hopes of ever getting married and tell yourself there are no good men available.
- The doctor tells you that you have an incurable disease so instead of believing God for total healing you resolve yourself to live on medication for the rest of your life and hope for the best.

Well my friend, God has great plans for you. He has made a promise to you in His word to give you the desires of your heart and to fulfill your dreams. That is, if you can believe. All things are possible to him who believes. It is possible to live debt-free, enjoy loving relationships, have a healthy body, own your home, be fulfilled in your career or operate a successful business. All of these things are possible and more.

How To Use This Journal

If you desire to live the abundant life, fulfill your dreams and do all the things that God has placed in your heart to do, there is a fool-proof secret to success found in the book of Joshua. In Joshua 1:8 God gave clear instructions on how one could do the impossible, become successful and live a prosperous life. He said *"This book of the law shall not depart out of your mouth, but you shall meditate on it day and night that you may observe to do all that is written in it. Then you will make yourself prosperous and then you shall have good success."* There you have it, "the secret to success."

This journal is designed to assist you in incorporating the principles of Joshua 1: 8. In the next 30 days you will be provided with a scripture, a confession of faith and a daily prayer. Each of them is designed to inspire your hope and build your faith in the word of God. These powerful scriptures will stir up your ability to dream bigger and increase your expectation of God to perform miracles in your life.

Make the three of these a part of your daily routine. Spend time meditating on the scriptures. Think on them throughout the day, let the word come alive and talk to you. Be consistent in planting the seeds of God's word in your heart. This will allow the reality of His willingness to do great things for you, to remove all of the doubt, fear and unbelief that has held you captive in the past. You will begin to see yourself and the obstacle around you differently and the light of God's truth will release His power in your life to do the impossible. The goal here is to recondition your heart to believe that anything is possible and that you can do, be or have anything His word says you can do, be or have.

During the next couple of weeks you will find your faith, hope and expectations increasing. You may also begin to hear the voice of God leading you. The Holy Spirit may speak to you in a number of different ways. He may start by answering questions you have concerning His word. He may give you new insight into a situation you have at home or work. God may nudge you to try something new or you may feel empowered to make a significant change in your life. Whatever you may experience know that it is all a part of your growing relationship with God and it is an important component in your journey towards your dreams.

So, for the next 30 days I challenge you. I challenge you to dream, dream and dream some more. Let your mind run free. Take the limits off your imagination. Remove all boundaries and inhibitions and expand yourself. Tell the Lord in the pages of this journal what you really want out of your life. Write it all down. Record everything. Read and meditate on your scriptures daily. Make your confessions at least three times a day. Obey the voice of God fearlessly. Press into God like never before. Talk to Him and let Him talk to you. And do it all with the knowledge that with God all things are possible and all things are possible to you if you can believe.

Happy Believing,

LaTania Michelle

Week 1

"Now to Him who is able to do exceedingly abundantly above all that we ask or think, according to the power that works in us...."

Ephesians 3:20

Take The Limits Off of God

"For I know the plans I have for you," declares the LORD, "plans to prosper you and not to harm you, plans to give you hope and a future." Jeremiah 29:11

T he success that God wants for you is far greater than the success you desire for yourself. His thoughts are higher than your thoughts and His ways are higher than your ways. God has plans for you to succeed and for you to have a happy and beautiful future. Even if you do have big dreams of achieving great things, you aspire to live the life style of the rich and famous or if you can see yourself starting a great movement and changing the world, God still wants more for you. More than you could ever imagine.

Have you ever noticed that God uses words like surpassing greatness, unlimited and exceeding when He talks about His love for you. He also uses words like abundance, plenteous and overflowing when He talks about how much He wants to bless you. Jesus said that He came to give you life and to give it to you more abundantly. In the amplified bible it reads this way "The thief comes only in order to steal and kill and destroy. I came that they may have and enjoy life, and have it in abundance (to the full, till it overflows)." Wow, what a personal mission statement Jesus gives here. He said that He came to mankind so that you could have life and enjoy it to the full.

So if this is the reason Christ gave as one of his objectives here on earth, why is it that so many Christians live unfulfilled joyless lives? I don't know, but I do know God has big dreams for you. He also has an amazing plan to fulfill your dreams. The problem is that He can't do any of those things until you begin to agree with Him and allow His dreams for you to become your dreams for yourself. God needs you to expand your thinking and take the limits off of what you believe He wants for you. Today God is asking you to begin to dream bigger than you ever have before and start reaching for stars. Don't be afraid, you can't out dream God. Remember Luke 1:37 says "...For with God nothing will be impossible."

Day 1

"..... for assuredly, I say to you, if you have faith as a mustard seed, you will say to this mountain, 'Move from here to there,' and it will move; and nothing will be impossible for you." Matthew 17:20

_____

_____

_____

_____

_____

_____

_____

_____

_____

_____

_____

_____

_____

_____

_____

_____

_____

_____

PRAYER FOR TODAY

Dear Heavenly Father, today I pray and ask you to help me dig up the dreams that I have hidden in my heart. Reveal to me those things that you have given to me to do and help me to become the person of faith that you have called me to be. Open my heart and my mind to the truth that with you all things are possible. In Jesus Name I pray. Amen

_____

_____

_____

_____

_____

ಐಂಡಐ

There are no limits to your possibilities. But the limits you place on your imagination.

ಐಂ ಡಐ

_____

_____

_____

_____

_____

_____

_____

_____

CONFESSION OF FAITH

I believe that God has great things planned for my life. I have faith to move mountains. Nothing shall be impossible for me today.

PRAYER NOTES

_____
_____
_____
_____
_____
_____
_____
_____
_____
_____
_____
_____
_____
_____
_____
_____
_____
_____
_____
_____
_____
_____
_____
_____

৪০য়৪

"Jesus said to him, 'If you can believe, all things are possible to him who believes'. " Mark 9:23

৪০য়৪

Day 2

"But He said, 'The things which are impossible with men are possible with God'." Luke 18:27

PRAYER FOR TODAY

Dear Heavenly Father, your word says that "The things which are impossible with men are possible with God. " I choose to believe your word over my circumstances today. I will not put my trust in men but I will trust in you and your word. I know that as long as I am with you nothing shall be impossible for me. Thank you Lord for your supernatural power that is at work in me. Thank you for your power that is turning things around in my life.

_____

_____

_____

_____

_____

_____

_____

_____

_____

_____

_____

_____

_____

_____

_____

CONFESSION OF FAITH

I place my confidence and trust in God, not man. I believe that things which are impossible for men are possible with God. Nothing is impossible for me because I believe.

PRAYER NOTES

_____

_____

_____

_____

_____

_____

_____

_____

_____

_____

_____

_____

_____

_____

_____

_____

_____

_____

_____

_____

_____

_____

_____

_____

_____

_____

&ЄЯ
"For with God nothing will be impossible." Luke 1:37
&ЄЯ

Day 3

"But without faith it is impossible to please Him, for he who comes to God must believe that He is, and that He is a rewarder of those who diligently seek Him."
Hebrews 11:6

PRAYER FOR TODAY

Dear Lord, thank you for the measure of faith that you have given me. I know that it makes you happy when I move in faith. Show me how to use my faith so that I can please you in all that I do today. Help me to believe in the impossible and to operate my faith to turn things around in my life and in the lives of others.

_____

_____

_____

_____

_____

_____

_____

_____

_____

ജ&ൽ

"Faith is the confidence, the assurance, the enforcing truth, the knowing...."
Robert Collier

ജ &ൽ

_____

_____

_____

_____

_____

CONFESSION OF FAITH

I believe that God rewards me because I seek him diligently. I am full of faith and I please God because I use my faith daily to believe for the impossible.

PRAYER NOTES

_____

_____

_____

_____

_____

_____

_____

_____

_____

_____

_____

_____

_____

_____

_____

_____

_____

_____

_____

_____

_____

_____

_____

ഇന്ദ്ര

"Jesus said to him, "If you can believe, all things are possible to him who believes." Mark 9:23

ഇന്ദ്ര

Day 4

"Is anything too hard for the Lord?..... ."
Genesis 18:14

_____
_____
_____
_____
_____
_____
_____
_____
_____
_____
_____
_____
_____
_____
_____
_____
_____
_____
_____
_____
_____
_____
_____
_____
_____
_____
_____

PRAYER FOR TODAY

Dear Lord, I know that nothing is too hard for you. I believe that you are bringing my impossible dreams to pass in my life. Just like Sarah, I have faith that causes me to give birth to every promise that you have given me. I love you Lord and I thank for your strength and wisdom to give birth to all of my dreams.

_____

_____

_____

_____

_____

_____

_____

ഇരുഃ

"Faith is the power to believe and the power to see."
Prentice Mulford

ഇരുഃ

_____

_____

_____

_____

_____

_____

CONFESSION OF FAITH

There is nothing too hard for God. I have faith that God is turning my impossible situations around and He is blessing me with every promise He has spoken to my heart.

PRAYER NOTES

_____

_____

_____

_____

_____

_____

_____

_____

_____

_____

_____

_____

_____

_____

_____

_____

_____

_____

_____

_____

_____

_____

_____

_____

ക്കരു
"For with God nothing will be impossible." Luke 1:37
ക്കരു

Day 5

"And He said, "Abba, Father, all things are possible for You. Take this cup away from Me; nevertheless, not what I will, but what You will."
Mark 14:36

_____

_____

_____

_____

_____

_____

_____

_____

_____

_____

_____

_____

_____

_____

_____

_____

_____

_____

_____

_____

_____

PRAYER FOR TODAY

Dear Heavenly Father. I know that all things are possible for you. Help me to understand the plan that you have for my life so that I can fulfill it to your glory. Work your divine plan in me so that your will for my life becomes the will that I have for myself. Strengthen me today, Lord, to do your will, express your joy and show your love wherever I may go.

_____

_____

_____

_____

_____

_____

_____

_____

_____

ഹെൽ

"Every man is a impossibility until he is broken."
Ralph Waldo Emerson

ഹെൽ

_____

_____

_____

_____

_____

CONFESSION OF FAITH

I will walk in the will of God for my life. I believe that with God all things are possible, therefore, it is possible for me to fulfill my destiny in Christ.

PRAYER NOTES

_____

_____

_____

_____

_____

_____

_____

_____

_____

_____

_____

_____

_____

_____

_____

_____

_____

_____

_____

_____

_____

_____

_____

_____

ഇൽൽ
"Jesus said to him, 'If you can believe, all things are possible to him who believes'." Mark 9:23
ഇൽൽ

Day 6

"Now it shall come to pass, if you diligently obey the voice of the Lord your God, to observe carefully all His commandments which I command you today, that the LORD your God will set you high above all nations of the earth." Deuteronomy 28:1

PRAYER FOR TODAY

Dear Lord, please help me to hear your voice more clearly and to have the courage to obey you fearlessly. Show me how to carefully observe your commands and to walk high above every situation in my life.

_____

_____

_____

_____

_____

_____

_____

_____
                      "The greater the

_____
      obstacle the more glory

_____
            in overcoming it."

_____
       Jean Baptiste Moliere

_____

_____

_____

_____

_____

_____

_____

_____

_____

CONFESSION OF FAITH

I hear the voice of God clearly and I am quick to obey everything that I hear Him speak to my heart.

PRAYER NOTES

ഇരുജ

"For with God nothing will be impossible." Luke 1:37

ഇരുജ

Day 7

"... According to your faith be it unto you." Matthew 9:29

PRAYER FOR TODAY

Dear Lord, thank you for the gift of faith that allows me to activate your miracle working power. I ask you now to show me how to use my faith in greater measure so that I can bring glory to your name.

_____

_____

_____

_____

_____

_____

_____   &)C&

_____   *"Don't believe in*
                                 miracles – depend
_____   *on them."*
                                  Laurence J. Peter
_____

                                     &)C&
_____

_____

_____

_____

_____

_____

_____

CONFESSION OF FAITH

According to my faith be it unto me. I am using my faith and activating the miracle working power of God in my life today.

PRAYER NOTES

_____

_____

_____

_____

_____

_____

_____

_____

_____

_____

_____

_____

_____

_____

_____

_____

_____

_____

_____

_____

_____

_____

_____

ജ൭ഝ
"For with God nothing will be impossible." Luke 1:37
ജ൭ഝ

Week 1

Write The Vision

"Then the LORD answered me and said: 'Write the vision, and make it plain on tablets, that he may run who reads it'." Habakkuk 2:2

Write your vision here. What has God revealed to you about your future this week? What promises has He spoken to your heart? What dream, vision or desire is He stirring up within your soul? List the promises you would like for God to fulfill in your life.

_____

_____

_____

_____

_____

_____

_____

_____

_____

_____

_____

_____

_____

Week 1

Journal of Blessings

"Be anxious for nothing, but in everything by prayer and supplication, with thanksgiving, let your requests be made known to God; and the peace of God, which surpasses all understanding, will guard your hearts and minds through Christ Jesus." Philippians 4:5-7

Take time to reflect on the goodness of God. List your blessings here and tell God how thankful you are for all that He has done for you this week.

_____

_____

_____

_____

_____

_____

_____

_____

_____

_____

_____

_____

Week 2

*"...But his delight is in the law
of the LORD,
and in His law he meditates
day and night.
He shall be like a tree
planted by the rivers of water,
that brings forth its fruit
in its season,
whose leaf also shall not wither;
and whatever he does
shall prosper."*

Psalm 1:2-3

Meditate On It Night And Day

"Keep this Book of the Law always on your lips; meditate on it day and night, so that you may be careful to do everything written in it. Then you will be prosperous and successful." Joshua 1:8

T houghts are powerful. What you focus your mind on you attract into your life. What you constantly think about you become. You cannot separate a person from the energy of their thoughts. This is the reason God tells us to think about or to meditate on His word night and day. Meditation is the key to transforming your thoughts from natural thinking to having the supernatural thoughts of God. By meditating on the word of God, you become convinced of His willingness and His ability to perform His promises in your life.

Learning to use your mind to focus on the promises of God is the initial step in changing your future for the better. Romans 12:2 says "... And do not be conformed to this world, but be transformed by the renewing of your mind, that you may prove what is that good and acceptable and perfect will of God."

Controlling your thoughts can be difficult, especially when you have developed the habit of thinking negatively about yourself, others or the world around you. But just like any other bad habit, it can be changed. Once you begin to take notice of your thoughts, you will start to see the thinking patterns that have framed the world in which you live. You can then make the conscious decision to use your thoughts to work for you and not against you. By meditating on the word of God, you are replacing your thoughts with God's thoughts and you start to think like God.

Whenever you are tempted to worry or dwell on a negative circumstance train yourself to shift your thoughts to the word of God. Think about, meditate on and imagine the promises of God. Meditate on one scripture each day or for several days until that scripture becomes alive within you. This will place you on the path to attracting God's promises and manifesting His supernatural love, peace and prosperity in your life. You will be amazed at the changes that will come from that single adjustment in your thinking.

Day 8

"May God himself, the God of peace, sanctify you through and through. May your whole spirit, soul and body be kept blameless at the coming of our Lord Jesus Christ." 1 Thessalonians 5:23

_____

_____

_____

_____

_____

_____

_____

_____

_____

_____

_____

_____

_____

_____

_____

_____

_____

PRAYER FOR TODAY

Dear Heavenly Father, I thank you for keeping my entire being, my spirit, my soul and my body blameless before you. I rest securely in your love for me and I am grateful that you are the God of peace. Please help me to reveal your peace to the world around me today.

_____

_____

_____

_____

_____

_____

_____

_____

_____

_____

_____

_____

_____

_____

_____

ଌଌ

"Faith is the confidence, the assurance, the enforcing truth, the knowing..."
Robert Collier

ଌଌ

_____

_____

_____

_____

CONFESSION OF FAITH

I am a spirit. I have a soul and I live in my body. My entire being is kept blameless and is set apart by God and I shall live in peace.

PRAYER NOTES

ℰᏜ
"For with God nothing will be impossible." Luke 1:37
ℰᏜ

37

Day 9

"As a man thinks in his heart so is he." Proverb 23:7

PRAYER FOR TODAY

Dear God, thank you for making me victorious in every area of my life. Thank you for giving me the ability to choose my thoughts. I choose to agree with your word and use my mind to think thoughts of victory today in Jesus Name.

_____

_____

_____

_____

_____

_____

_____

_____

_____

_____

_____

_____

_____

_____

_____

_____

℘ℭ℞

"A man is what he believes."
Anton Chekhov

℘ℭ℞

CONFESSION OF FAITH

I have the ability to change my world by the things I choose to think. I will think loving thoughts filled with peace and joy today. Therefore I will have love, peace and joy in my life.

PRAYER NOTES

_____

_____

_____

_____

_____

_____

_____

_____

_____

_____

_____

_____

_____

_____

_____

_____

_____

_____

_____

_____

_____

_____

_____

_____

ഩരാ

"Jesus said to him, 'If you can believe, all things are possible to him who believes'." Mark 9:23

ഩരാ

Day 10

"*Behold I have given you authority and power to trample upon serpents and scorpions and over all power and that the enemy possess and nothing shall in any way harm you.*" Luke 10: 19

_____
_____
_____
_____
_____
_____
_____
_____
_____
_____
_____
_____
_____
_____
_____
_____
_____
_____
_____
_____
_____

PRAYER FOR TODAY

Dear Heavenly Father, thank you for giving us your son Jesus. Jesus, thank you for giving us power and authority over every work of the enemy. Help me to understand this authority and to use it fearlessly in a manner that glorifies you.

_____

_____

_____

_____

_____

_____

_____

_____   ∞∞

_____   *"Within you right*

_____   *now is the power to*

_____   *do things you never*

_____   *dreamed possible.*

_____   *This power becomes*

_____   *available to you just*

_____   *as soon as you can*

_____   *change your*

_____   *beliefs."*

_____   **Maxwell Maltz**

_____   ∞∞

_____

_____

CONFESSION OF FAITH

Nothing can harm me or hurt me today because Christ has given me authority and power over all the works of the enemy.

PRAYER NOTES

_____

_____

_____

_____

_____

_____

_____

_____

_____

_____

_____

_____

_____

_____

_____

_____

_____

_____

_____

_____

_____

_____

_____

_____

_____

 හ෴ශ
"For with God nothing will be impossible." Luke 1:37
හ෴ශ

Day 11

"Rejoice not against me, O mine enemy: when I fall, I shall arise; when I sit in darkness, the LORD shall be a light unto me." Micah 7:8

_____

_____

_____

_____

_____

_____

_____

_____

_____

_____

_____

_____

_____

_____

_____

_____

_____

_____

_____

_____

_____

_____

_____

PRAYER FOR TODAY

Dear Lord, thank for always a being a light in my time of darkness and a strong hand to lift me when I fall. Help me to walk confidently today, knowing that you are always with me. And you will always help me whenever I call on you.

_____

_____

_____

_____

_____

_____

_____

_____

_____

_____

ℰℭ

"Faith is the power to believe and the power to see...."
Prentice Mulford

ℰℭ

_____

_____

_____

_____

_____

_____

_____

CONFESSION OF FAITH

I declare that whenever I fall I will immediately get right back up. Nothing can keep me down and no enemy can defeat me.

PRAYER NOTES

_____

_____

_____

_____

_____

_____

_____

_____

_____

_____

_____

_____

_____

_____

_____

_____

_____

_____

_____

_____

_____

_____

ⅧⅣ

"Jesus said to him, 'If you can believe, all things are possible to him who believes'." Mark 9:23

ⅧⅣ

Day 12

"Most assuredly, I say to you, he who believes in Me, the works that I do he will do also; and greater works than these he will do, because I go to My Father." John 14:12

_____

_____

_____

_____

_____

_____

_____

_____

_____

_____

_____

_____

_____

_____

_____

_____

_____

_____

_____

_____

PRAYER FOR TODAY

Dear Heavenly Father, thank you for the power that you have given me through your son Jesus Christ to do great works in the earth. Help me today Lord God to be your vessel in the earth and do greater works all to your glory.

_____

_____

_____

_____

_____

_____

_____

_____

_____

_____

_____

_____

_____

_____

_____

_____

_____

CONFESSION OF FAITH

I declare that Jesus Christ is Lord. I will do great things in life because I believe in Christ Jesus.

PRAYER NOTES

_____

_____

_____

_____

_____

_____

_____

_____

_____

_____

_____

_____

_____

_____

_____

_____

_____

_____

_____

_____

_____

_____

_____

_____

ಐಲ

"For with God nothing will be impossible." Luke 1:37

ಐ ಲ

Day 13

"And we know that all things work together for good to those who love God, to those who are the called according to His purpose."
Romans 8:28

_____

_____

_____

_____

_____

_____

_____

_____

_____

_____

_____

_____

_____

_____

_____

_____

_____

_____

_____

_____

PRAYER FOR TODAY

Dear Lord, thank you for working out everything perfectly in my life. I know that you are turning things around for my good, so I will trust you completely and continue to focus on walking in my divine purpose.

_____

_____

_____

_____

_____

_____

_____   ଞ୬ଈ

_____   *"There are no gains*
                                    without pains."
_____   **Benjamin Franklin**

_____   ଞ୬ଈ

_____

_____

_____

_____

_____

_____

_____

CONFESSION OF FAITH

I love God and I walk continually according to His divine purpose for my life.

PRAYER NOTES

ഇരു

"For with God nothing will be impossible." Luke 1:37

ഇരു

Day 14

"While we do not look at the things which are seen, but at the things which are not seen. For the things which are seen are temporary, but the things which are not seen are eternal." II Corinthians 4: 18

_____
_____
_____
_____
_____
_____
_____
_____
_____
_____
_____
_____
_____
_____
_____
_____
_____
_____
_____
_____
_____

PRAYER FOR TODAY

Dear Lord, please help me to walk by faith and not by sight. Allow me to focus on the things which I see in your word and not the things that I see with my eyes. Help me to understand eternal truth and to live by it.

_____

_____

_____

_____

_____

_____

_____

_____

_____

_____

_____

_____

ഏ൦ൻ

"The only thing that stands between a man and what he wants in life is often merely the will to try it and the faith to believe that it is possible."
Richard M. DeVos

ഏ൦ൻ

_____

_____

_____

CONFESSION OF FAITH

I walk by faith and not by sight.

54

PRAYER NOTES

_____

_____

_____

_____

_____

_____

_____

_____

_____

_____

_____

_____

_____

_____

_____

_____

_____

_____

_____

_____

_____

_____

_____

ഐൽ

"For with God nothing will be impossible." Luke 1:37

ഇൽ

Week 2

Write The Vision

"Then the LORD answered me and said: 'Write the vision, and make it plain on tablets, that he may run who reads it'." Habakkuk 2:2

Write your vision here. What has God revealed to you about your future this week. What promises has He spoken to your heart? What dream, vision or desire is He stirring up within your soul? List the promises you would like for God to fulfill in your life.

_____

_____

_____

_____

_____

_____

_____

_____

_____

_____

_____

_____

_____

Week 2

Journal of Blessings

"Be anxious for nothing, but in everything by prayer and supplication, with thanksgiving, let your requests be made known to God; and the peace of God, which surpasses all understanding, will guard your hearts and minds through Christ Jesus." Philippians 4:5-7

Take time to reflect on the goodness of God. List your blessings here and tell God how thankful you are for all that He has done for you this week.

_____

_____

_____

_____

_____

_____

_____

_____

_____

_____

_____

_____

Week 3

"... For out of the abundance of the heart the mouth speaks.
A good man out of the good treasure of his heart brings forth good things, and an evil man out of the evil treasure brings forth evil things.
But I say to you that for every idle word men may speak, they will give account of it in the day of judgment. For by your words you will be justified, and by your words you will be condemned."

Matthew 12:34-37

Confessions of Faith

"Keep this Book of the Law always on your lips; meditate on it day and night, so that you may be careful to do everything written in it. Then you will be prosperous and successful." Joshua 1:8

A faith confession is a positive statement made in agreement with God's word. It does not take into consideration the circumstance. It declares the desired outcome as a fact. Remember you are like God. You were created to be a speaking spirit. You were created to transform your environment by the power of your words. When the words you speak line up with the words that God has already spoken about you, then you can be like God and boldly call those things that are not as though they were. With your confession of faith you are acting like God and you then become the God over your situation. It doesn't matter how hopeless things may seem. There is power to turn things around when you use a faith confession.

The confession of faith is crucial to the manifestation of your prayers. Jesus told His disciples "For assuredly, I say to you, whoever says to this mountain, 'Be removed and be cast into the sea,' and does not doubt in his heart, but believes that those things he says will be done, he will have whatever he says. Therefore, I say to you, whatever things you ask when you pray, believe that you receive *them,* and you will have *them."* Mark 11:23-27

In this passage Jesus uses the word say or says four times and uses the word prays one time. This lets me know that we should be speaking words of faith over circumstances at least four times as much as we pray over them. Training yourself to make your faith confession several times a day is very important. Romans 10:7 say that faith comes by hearing and hearing by the word of God. The more you confess the word of God over your circumstances the greater your faith will become. The greater your faith becomes the more the impossible seem to look possible. No matter what your situation may look like today, you can turn it around with your confession of faith. Remember, God created this world with his words and you too can create your world with your words.

Day 15

*"For I know the thoughts that I think towards you, says the LORD,
thoughts of peace and not of evil, to give you a future and a hope."*
Jeremiah 29:11

PRAYER FOR TODAY

Dear Lord, I want to thank you for the wonderful plan you have for my life. Thank you for giving me the Holy Spirit who leads me into all truth. Make your plans for me alive in my heart so that I may walk in them courageously today.

_____

_____

_____

_____

_____

_____

_____ ଚଚଚ

_____ *"If we all did the things*
we are capable of doing,
_____ *we would literally*
astound ourselves."
_____ **Thomas A. Edison**

_____ ଚଚଚ

_____

_____

_____

_____

_____

CONFESSION OF FAITH

God has a good plan for me. God is planning to do me good and not evil all the days of my life. I trust the Lord to give me a good future.

PRAYER NOTES

_____
_____
_____
_____
_____
_____
_____
_____
_____
_____
_____
_____
_____
_____
_____
_____
_____
_____
_____
_____
_____
_____
_____

ༀ

"Jesus said to him, 'If you can believe, all things are possible to him who believes'." Mark 9:23

ༀ

Day 16

"But you shall receive power when the Holy Spirit has come upon you; and you shall be witnesses to Me in Jerusalem, and in all Judea and Samaria, and to the end of the earth." Acts 1:8

PRAYER FOR TODAY

Dear Heavenly Father, thank you for the gift of the Holy Spirit and for the power of God that is within me. Show me how to be a greater witness for you and to use this power with wisdom and grace according to your will.

_____

_____

_____

_____

_____

_____

_____

_____

_____

_____

_____

_____

_____

_____

"While there is life, there's hope."
Marcus Tullius Cicero

CONFESSION OF FAITH

I am filled with the Holy Spirit and I have the supernatural power of God living in me today. I have the power to be an extra ordinary witness for Christ everywhere I go because the Spirit of God lives in me.

PRAYER NOTES

80CR

"For with God nothing will be impossible." Luke 1:37

80CR

Day 17

"Two are better than one because they have a good return for their labor. For if either of them falls, the one will lift up his companion. But woe to the one who falls when there is not another to lift him up. Furthermore, if two lie down together they keep warm, but how can one be warm alone?" Ecclesiastes 4:9-11

PRAYER FOR TODAY

Dear Heavenly Father, help me to be connected to the people that you have chosen for my life. Remove all others from my heart, mind and atmosphere. Give me wisdom to make friends with true believers and be a good friend to them for your glory.

_____

_____

_____

_____

_____

ഓൽ

_____

"You can do anything
you wish to do, have
anything you wish to
have, be anything you
wish to be."
Robert Collier

ഓൽ

_____

_____

_____

_____

_____

_____

CONFESSION OF FAITH

I am connected with godly companions. The Lord fills my life with good friends and we are a blessing to each others lives.

PRAYER NOTES

Day 18

"Now to Him who is able to do exceedingly abundantly above all that we ask or think, according to the power that works in us."
Ephesians 3:20

PRAYER FOR TODAY

Dear Lord, your word says that you are able to do exceedingly abundantly above all that I can ask or think. Please raise my expectation for what you can and will do in my life so I can receive the best you have for me. Teach me to use the power that is at work in me to receive great and wonderful things from you today.

_____

_____

_____

_____

_____

_____

_____   ℛℭ

_____   *"It is only with the heart*

_____   *that one can see rightly;*

_____   *what is essential is*

_____   *invisible to the eye."*

_____   ***Antoine De Saint-Exupery***

                                       ℛℭ

_____

_____

_____

_____

_____

_____

CONFESSION OF FAITH

I will raise my expectation and expect God to do big things in my life today.

PRAYER NOTES

_____

_____

_____

_____

_____

_____

_____

_____

_____

_____

_____

_____

_____

_____

_____

_____

_____

_____

_____

_____

_____

_____

_____

ऊ०क्ष
"For with God nothing will be impossible." Luke 1:37
ऊ०क्ष

Day 19

"Beloved, I pray that you may prosper in all things and be in health, just as your soul prospers." 3 John1:2

PRAYER FOR TODAY

Dear Lord, give me grace to stay in your word and learn from it so that I can prosper my soul. I know that it is your will to prosper me and to heal me. So I receive all of your blessings in my life today by faith in perfect and miraculous ways.

_____

_____

_____

_____

_____

_____   ಐಂಬ

_____   *"Action Conquers Fear."*
                                         Peter Nivio Zarlenga
_____   ಐಂಬ

_____

_____

_____

_____

_____

_____

CONFESSION OF FAITH

God wishes above all things that I prosper and be in health even as my soul prospers.

PRAYER NOTES

_____
_____
_____
_____
_____
_____
_____
_____
_____
_____
_____
_____
_____
_____
_____
_____
_____
_____
_____
_____
_____
_____
_____
_____

ഽറൌ

"Jesus said to him, 'If you can believe, all things are possible to him who believes'. " Mark 9:23

ഽറൌ

Day 20

"But seek first the kingdom of God and His righteousness, and all these things shall be added to you." Matthew 6:33

_____

_____

_____

_____

_____

_____

_____

_____

_____

_____

_____

_____

_____

_____

_____

_____

_____

_____

_____

_____

_____

_____

PRAYER FOR TODAY

Dear Heavenly Father, thank you for your promise to give me everything I need as I put you first in my life and learn to live by your plan of righteousness.

_____

_____

_____

_____

_____

_____

_____

_____

_____

_____

_____

80Q03

"While there is life, there's hope."
Marcus Tullius Cicero

80C03

_____

_____

_____

_____

_____

CONFESSION OF FAITH

God takes care of all my needs because I seek first the kingdom of God.

PRAYER NOTES

_____

_____

_____

_____

_____

_____

_____

_____

_____

_____

_____

_____

_____

_____

_____

_____

_____

_____

_____

_____

_____

_____

_____

_____

_____

_____

ഇൻ

"For with God nothing will be impossible." Luke 1:37

ഇൻ

Day 21

"And since we have the same spirit of faith, according to what is written, 'I believed and therefore I spoke', we also believe and therefore speak." II Corinthians 4:13

_____
_____
_____
_____
_____
_____
_____
_____
_____
_____
_____
_____
_____
_____
_____
_____
_____
_____
_____
_____
_____
_____
_____

PRAYER FOR TODAY

Dear Lord, thank you for the spirit of faith that you have placed in my heart. Holy Spirit help me to always speak with faith and not the doubt that may be in my mind. Help me Spirit of God to stay focused on all of the wonderful things that you are doing in my life and not on the negative circumstances that are around me.

_____

_____

_____

_____

_____

_____

ക്കൗ

"No pain, no palm; no thorns; no throne; no gall; no glory; no cross; no crown."
William Penn

_____

_____

_____

_____

_____

_____

CONFESSION OF FAITH

I have the Spirit of faith. I believe the word of God and I speak it continually. I refuse to look at my natural circumstances, but I choose to look on the unseen blessings that I know God has for me.

PRAYER NOTES

_____

_____

_____

_____

_____

_____

_____

_____

_____

_____

_____

_____

_____

_____

_____

_____

_____

_____

_____

_____

_____

_____

ଞଓଚଃ

"Jesus said to him, 'If you can believe, all things are possible to him who believes'." Mark 9:23

ଞଓଚଃ

Week 3

Write The Vision

"Then the LORD answered me and said: 'Write the vision, and make it plain on tablets, that he may run who reads it'." Habakkuk 2:2

Write your vision here. What has God revealed to you about your future this week? What promises has he spoken to your heart? What dream, vision or desire is He stirring up within your soul? List the promises you find in the word that relates to your desire.

_____

_____

_____

_____

_____

_____

_____

_____

_____

_____

_____

_____

_____

Week 3

Journal of Blessings

"Be anxious for nothing, but in everything by prayer and supplication, with thanksgiving, let your requests be made known to God; and the peace of God, which surpasses all understanding, will guard your hearts and minds through Christ Jesus." Philippians 4:5-7

Take time to reflect on the goodness of God. List your Blessings here and tell God how thankful you are for all that He has done for you this week.

_____

_____

_____

_____

_____

_____

_____

_____

_____

_____

_____

_____

Week 4

" If you know these things,
blessed are you if you do them."

John 13:17

Blessings For Those Who Do The Word

T he blessings of God come to those who do the word and not just hear the word. So, it is vitally important that you purpose in your heart and make a quality decision to be a doer of the word. That means to do the things that you read in the word as well as being obedient to the voice of the Lord you hear speaking to your heart. Here are a few scriptures that refer to the blessings that come to those who make a practice of doing the word.

James 1:22-25
But be doers of the word, and not hearers only, deceiving yourselves. For if anyone is a hearer of the word and not a doer, he is like a man observing his natural face in a mirror; for he observes himself, goes away, and immediately forgets what kind of man he was. But he who looks into the perfect law of liberty and continues in it, and is not a forgetful hearer but a doer of the work, this one will be blessed in what he does.

Deuteronomy 28:1-14
And it shall come to pass, if thou shall hearken diligently unto the voice of the LORD thy God, to observe and to do all his commandments which I command thee this day, that the LORD thy God will set thee on high above all nations of the earth:

And all these blessings shall come on thee, and overtake thee, if thou shall hearken unto the voice of the LORD thy God. Blessed shall thou be in the city, and blessed shall thou be in the field.   Blessed shall be the fruit of thy body, and the fruit of thy ground, and the fruit of thy cattle, the increase of thy kine, and the flocks of thy sheep. Blessed shall be thy basket and thy store. Blessed shall thou be when thou come in, and blessed shall thou be when thou go out. The LORD shall cause your enemies that rise up against thee to be smitten before thy face: they shall come out against thee one way, and flee before thee seven ways. The LORD shall command the blessing upon thee in thy storehouses, and in all that thou sets your hand unto; and he shall bless thee in the land which the LORD thy God gives thee.

Day 22

"Christ has redeemed us from the curse of the law, having become a curse for us, for it is written, "Cursed is everyone who hangs on a tree", that the blessing of Abraham might come upon the Gentiles in Christ Jesus, that we might receive the promise of the Spirit through faith." Galatians 3:13-14

PRAYER FOR TODAY

Dear Heavenly Father, thank you for the redemption I have because of the work Jesus Christ did on the cross for me. Thank you for the blessing of Abraham that is now mine. Thank you for the spirit of faith that you have given me so that I can have your blessings in my life.

_____

_____

_____

_____

_____

_____

ജ്ഞ

_____   *"Faith is the power*
to believe and the
_____   *power to see..."*
Prentice Mulford
_____   ജ്ഞ

_____

_____

_____

_____

_____

CONFESSION OF FAITH

Christ has redeemed me from the curse of the law, being made a curse for me. I receive the promise of the Spirit through faith because I am Abraham's seed. Through Jesus, I am an heir of the blessings of Abraham.

PRAYER NOTES

_____

_____

_____

_____

_____

_____

_____

_____

_____

_____

_____

_____

_____

_____

_____

_____

_____

_____

_____

_____

_____

_____

_____

_____

_____

_____

_____

ഇ രു

"For with God nothing will be impossible." Luke 1:37

ഇ രു

Day 23

"Now may the God of hope fill you with all joy and peace in believing,
that ye may abound in hope through the power of the Holy Spirit."
Romans 15:13

_____

_____

_____

_____

_____

_____

_____

_____

_____

_____

_____

_____

_____

_____

_____

_____

_____

_____

_____

_____

_____

_____

PRAYER FOR TODAY

Dear Heavenly Father, thank you for the force of hope that you have given to me through the power of the Holy Spirit. Help me to remain filled with peace and joy as I continue to have faith for you to do the impossible in my life. Let hope abound in my heart as I look with expectation for you to do great things in my life.

_____

_____

_____

_____

_____

_____

_____   ෩෩

_____   *"Life in abundance*
                             comes only through
_____   *great love. ..."*

_____   ෩෩

_____

_____

_____

_____

_____

CONFESSION OF FAITH

I am filled with the Holy Spirit of God. Hope is abounding in my life. I have peace that God is bringing the desires of my heart to pass and I will express the joy of the Lord with everyone I encounter today.

PRAYER NOTES

_____
_____
_____
_____
_____
_____
_____
_____
_____
_____
_____
_____
_____
_____
_____
_____
_____
_____
_____
_____
_____
_____
_____
_____
_____
_____

ഇൻ

"Jesus said to him, 'If you can believe, all things are possible to him who believes'." Mark 9:23

ഇൻ

Day 24

"Then Jesus said to those Jews who believed Him, 'If you abide in My word, you are My disciples indeed. And you shall know the truth, and the truth shall make you free'." John 8:31-32

PRAYER FOR TODAY

Dear Lord, thank you for the freedom that I have in you. Thank you for your word that is alive and living inside of me. Please help me to abide in your word and to be the disciple that you have called me to be. Thank you for your truth that sets me free. Guide me Holy Spirit into the place of freedom you have for me today.

_____

_____

_____

_____

_____

_____

_____   ∞∝

_____   *"It is only with the heart
                                   that one can see rightly
_____   what is essential is
                                    invisible to the eye."*
_____   ***Antoine De Saint-Exupery***

_____   ∞∝

_____

_____

_____

_____

CONFESSION OF FAITH

I am a disciple of Christ and I am abiding in the word of God. I declare that I am free from the bondage of the enemy and nothing is impossible for me today.

PRAYER NOTES

_____
_____
_____
_____
_____
_____
_____
_____
_____
_____
_____
_____
_____
_____
_____
_____
_____
_____
_____
_____
_____
_____

৪১৫৪

"For with God nothing will be impossible." Luke 1:37

৪১৫৪

Day 25

"It is the Spirit who gives life; the flesh profits nothing. The words
that I speak to you are spirit, and they are life."
John 6:63

PRAYER FOR TODAY

Dear Heavenly Father, thank you for your word that is living in me. Help me to move by your Spirit today to bring your life to the world.

_____
_____
_____
_____
_____
_____

_____

_____   ℬↄ☾ℛ

_____   *"A wise man has*

_____   *great power, and a*

_____   *man of knowledge*

_____   *increases strength."*
                                          Proverbs 24:5
_____
                                            ℬↄ☾ℛ
_____

_____
_____
_____
_____
_____
_____
_____

CONFESSION OF FAITH

I have the word of God in me therefore the Spirit of God and the Life of God lives in me too.

PRAYER NOTES

_____

_____

_____

_____

_____

_____

_____

_____

_____

_____

_____

_____

_____

_____

_____

_____

_____

_____

_____

_____

 හිතු

"For with God nothing will be impossible." Luke 1:37

 හිතු

Day 26

"But you shall receive power when the Holy Spirit has come upon you; and you shall be witnesses to Me in Jerusalem, and in all Judea and Samaria, and to the end of the earth." Acts 1:8

PRAYER FOR TODAY

Thank You Heavenly Father, for Your Holy Spirit. Thank you for the power you have given to me to be a witness for you. Help me today Lord to walk in your power and acknowledge your presence. Help me to be more like you and do the impossible.

_____

_____

_____

_____

_____

_____

_____

_____

_____

_____

_____

_____

_____

ജ൩ര
"Life is largely a matter of expectation."
Horace
ജ൩ര

_____

_____

_____

_____

_____

CONFESSION OF FAITH

I am a powerful witness for the kingdom of God today because the Holy Spirit lives in me.

PRAYER NOTES

_____

_____

_____

_____

_____

_____

_____

_____

_____

_____

_____

_____

_____

_____

_____

_____

_____

_____

_____

_____

_____

_____

_____

_____

ഇൗൽ

"For with God nothing will be impossible." Luke 1:37

ഇൗൽ

Day 27

"...and to ask that you may be filled with the knowledge of His will in all wisdom and spiritual understanding; that you may walk worthy of the Lord, fully pleasing Him, being fruitful in every good work and increasing in the knowledge of God." Colossians 1:9-10

_____

_____

_____

_____

_____

_____

_____

_____

_____

_____

_____

_____

_____

_____

_____

_____

_____

_____

_____

_____

_____

_____

PRAYER FOR TODAY

Thank You Heavenly Father, for filling me with the knowledge of your will in all wisdom and spiritual understanding. I have faith that you are revealing to me all that I need to know so that I can walk worthy of you and be fruitful in all that I do.

_____

_____

_____

_____

_____

_____

_____

_____

_____

_____

_____

_____

_____

_____

CONFESSION OF FAITH

I am filled with the knowledge of God's will for my life. I walk in wisdom and spiritual understanding today and I am increasing in my knowledge of God in every way.

PRAYER NOTES

_____

_____

_____

_____

_____

_____

_____

_____

_____

_____

_____

_____

_____

_____

_____

_____

_____

_____

_____

_____

_____

_____

_____

_____

_____

_____

ഓര

"Jesus said to him, 'If you can believe, all things are possible to him who believes'." Mark 9:23

ഓര

Week 4

Write The Vision

"Then the LORD answered me and said: 'Write the vision, and make it plain on tablets, that he may run who reads it'." Habakkuk 2:2

Write your vision here. What has God revealed to you about your future this week? What promises has He spoken to your heart? What dream, vision or desire is He stirring up within your soul? List the promises you find in the word that relates to your desire.

_____

_____

_____

_____

_____

_____

_____

_____

_____

_____

_____

_____

_____

Week 4

Journal of Blessings

"Be anxious for nothing, but in everything by prayer and supplication, with thanksgiving, let your requests be made known to God; and the peace of God, which surpasses all understanding, will guard your hearts and minds through Christ Jesus." Philippians 4:5-7

Take time to reflect on the goodness of God. List your blessings here and tell God how thankful you are for all that He has done for you this week.

_____

_____

_____

_____

_____

_____

_____

_____

_____

_____

_____

_____

Day 28

"Therefore, if anyone is in Christ, he is a new creation; old things have passed away; behold, all things have become new. Now all things are of God, who has reconciled us to Himself through Jesus Christ, and has given us the ministry of reconciliation."
II Corinthians 5: 17-18

PRAYER FOR TODAY

Thank you, Lord for this new day. Help me to see myself as you see me. Make me alive to my new identity in Christ. Fill me with your Spirit so that I can be transformed into my new image.

_____
_____
_____
_____
_____
_____
_____

ജ൯൞

"Seek not to understand that you may believe but believe that you may understand."
Saint Augustine

ജ൯൞

_____
_____
_____
_____

CONFESSION OF FAITH

I am a new creature in Christ Jesus. All of my past mistakes have passed away and I have become new.

PRAYER NOTES

_____
_____
_____
_____
_____
_____
_____
_____
_____
_____
_____
_____
_____
_____
_____
_____
_____
_____
_____
_____
_____
_____
_____
_____
_____
_____
_____
_____

ಕಾ

"For with God nothing will be impossible." Luke 1:37

ಕಾ

Day 29

"For the word of God is living and powerful, and sharper than any two-edged sword, piercing even to the division of soul and spirit, and of joints and marrow, and is a discerner of the thoughts and intents of the heart." Hebrews 4:12

PRAYER FOR TODAY

Dear Heavenly Father, thank you for the powerful, active living word of God that you have given me. I believe that your word is true and that it is alive in me now. Help me to receive and understand your word so that I can make changes in my heart that will manifest your promises in my life.

_____

_____

_____

_____

_____

_____

_____

_____

_____

_____

_____

_____

_____

_____

_____

_____

_____

_____

_____

CONFESSION OF FAITH

The powerful, active living word of God is always on my lips. I mediate on it every day and as a result I am prosperous and successful.

PRAYER NOTES

_____
_____
_____
_____
_____
_____
_____
_____
_____
_____
_____
_____
_____
_____
_____
_____
_____
_____
_____
_____
_____
_____

ಹೃಂ

"Jesus said to him, 'If you can believe, all things are possible to him who believes'." Mark 9:23

ಹೃಂ

Day 30

"This Book of the Law shall not depart from your mouth, but you shall meditate in it day and night, that you may observe to do according to all that is written in it. For then you will make your way prosperous, and then you will have good success." Joshua 1:8

_____
_____
_____
_____
_____
_____
_____
_____
_____
_____
_____
_____
_____
_____
_____
_____
_____
_____
_____
_____
_____

PRAYER FOR TODAY

Heavenly Father, thank you for revealing to me your formula for success. Help me to always make your word the final authority in my life. Help me to read your word, think about your word, and speak your word so that I can be a doer of it. Show me how to do impossible things through your word today.

_____

_____

_____

_____

_____

_____

_____

_____

_____ ୫୬୦୪

_____ *"Faith is the power*

_____ *to believe and the*

_____ *power to see."*

_____ *Prentice Mulford*

_____ ୫୬ ୦୪

_____

_____

_____

_____

_____

CONFESSION OF FAITH

I love the word of God. I meditate on it, speak it and do it. As such, I am prosperous and successful in all that I do today.

114

PRAYER NOTES

_____

_____

_____

_____

_____

_____

_____

_____

_____

_____

_____

_____

_____

_____

_____

_____

_____

_____

_____

_____

_____

_____

_____

_____

ಐುಲ
"Jesus said to him, 'If you can believe, all things are possible to him who believes'." Mark 9:23
ಐ ಲ

Week 5

Write The Vision

"Then the LORD answered me and said: 'Write the vision, and make it plain on tablets, that he may run who reads it'." *Habakkuk 2:2*

Write your vision here. What has God revealed to you about your future this week? What promises has He spoken to your heart? What dream, vision or desire is He stirring up within your soul? List the promises you find in the word that relate to your desire.

_____

_____

_____

_____

_____

_____

_____

_____

_____

_____

_____

_____

Week 5

Journal of Blessings

"Be anxious for nothing, but in everything by prayer and supplication, with thanksgiving, let your requests be made known to God; and the peace of God, which surpasses all understanding, will guard your hearts and minds through Christ Jesus." Philippians 4:5-7

Take time to reflect on the goodness of God. List your blessings here and tell God how thankful you are for all that He has done for you this week.

_____

_____

_____

_____

_____

_____

_____

_____

_____

_____

_____

PERSONAL INVITATION

I If you are reading this and realize you have never accepted God's offer of salvation in Jesus Christ or if you simply are not sure if you are a part of the family of God I invite you to receive Jesus Christ into your life today. Pray this prayer by faith right now.

Heavenly Father, I come to you in the Name of Jesus. Your word says, *Whosoever shall call on the name of the Lord shall be saved"* (Acts 2:21). I am calling on you now. I pray and ask Jesus to come into my heart and be Lord over my life according to Romans 10:9-10. *"If thou shall confess with thy mouth the Lord Jesus, and shall believe in your heart that God hath raised him from the dead, thou shall be saved. For with the heart man believeth unto righteousness; and with the mouth confession is made unto salvation."* I do that now. I confess that Jesus is Lord, and I believe in my heart that God raised Him from the dead.

I am now reborn! I am a Christian. I am now a child of God! Heavenly Father you also said in Your Word, *"If ye then, being evil, know how to give good gifts unto your children: HOW MUCH MORE shall your Heavenly Father give the Holy Spirit to them that ask him?"* (Luke 11:13). I'm also asking You to fill me with the Holy Spirit. Holy Spirit, rise up within me as I praise God. I fully expect to speak with other tongues as You give me the utterance (Acts 2:4).

Begin to praise God for filling you with the Holy Spirit. Speak out of your mouth the words and syllables you receive from your spirit. This is not your natural language but the language given to you by the Holy Spirit. The Spirit of God will not force you to speak but will guide you gently in your spirit, to use your voice, to speak his words.

Now that you have Jesus as your savoir and you are filled with the Holy Spirit begin to pray and worship God daily in your new heavenly language. This will enhance you in your new relationship with God, His Son Jesus and the Holy Spirit.

Welcome to the family of God.

My Impossible Dream

_____

_____

_____

_____

_____

_____

_____

_____

_____

_____

_____

_____

_____

_____

_____

_____

_____

_____

_____

_____

_____

Sign and Date

ABOUT THE AUTHOR

LaTania Michelle knows about facing impossibilities. Her experiences as a business woman, minister, mentor, coach, mother and friend has given her an insight into what it takes to overcome great obstacles and turn impossibilities into possibilities. As the Founder of the Wealthy Woman's Network, LaTania has touched the lives of many across the country and overseas with a passion for releasing the unlimited potential that lies within.

LaTania is the recipient of a number of awards for both business and ministry including: The Life Time Achievement Award from the Crenshaw Christian Center, The Goodwill Industries Business Now Training Award as well as recognition and honors from the City of Los Angeles, the California State Assembly and the California State Senate.

LaTania now speaks on a variety of topics inspiring others to live a life of Passion, Purpose and Prosperity. For more information on how you can book LaTania for your business, organization or ministry e-mail her at latania.smith@gmail.com.

ഇഐ

Are you looking for more inspiration and spiritual support to help you build your faith and follow your dreams?

Subscribe to the Possibility Factor Newsletter.
The Possibility Factor Newsletter is published monthly and designed to give you a regular dose of the information, inspiration and revelation needed to lead you to your wealthy place in the kingdom of God.

This FREE online publication provides you with the opportunity to:

- Be invited to FREE tele-seminars that help you achieve your goals and stay spiritually grounded.
- Connect with other spirit-filled, like minded women
- Receive educational and motivational articles for spiritual and professional enrichment.
- And much more!

Subscribe today to receive your Free Possibility Factor Newsletter and receive your free a chapter of the on-line "Possibility Factor."

To learn more and sign up now, visit
www.possibilityfactor.com

෨෨

"Again I say to you that if two of you agree on earth concerning anything that they ask, it will be done for them by My Father in heaven."

Would you like for us to agree with
you in prayer for your
impossible dreams?

Join LaTania Michelle and other powerful prayer
warriors for intercessory prayer by phone
every Saturday at 10am pst.
Call (605)475-4875
Code 578545#.

You can also mail your
prayer request, testimonials, donation or comments to
LaTania Michelle Smith
3940 Marine Ave. Suite #A
Lawndale, Ca 90260

෨෨

৪৩৫৩

Connect With LaTania Michelle Online

To Find Out More

About LaTania Michelle's Upcoming Events

Watch LaTania Michelle On Video

Share Your Impossible Dream

Find Impossible Dream Partners

Get Resources To Deepen Your Faith

And Much More

Go to www.possibilityfactor.com

Coming Soon By LaTania Michelle

The Possibility Factor,
Your Guide To Believing Anything
is Possible For You
And

Faith For Your Mate

৪৩৫৩

www.ingramcontent.com/pod-product-compliance
Lightning Source LLC
Chambersburg PA
CBHW060436090426
42733CB00011B/2295